INSIDE ANCIENT
ROME

by L. L. Owens

Perfection Learning®

Incubator Grant 16.01

About the Author

Lisa L. Owens grew up in the Midwest. She has been writing since she was a little girl, and she has always loved to learn about people and cultures from all periods in history.

She currently works as an editor and writer in Seattle, where she lives with her husband, Timothy Johnson.

Other books by Ms. Owens include *Brothers at War*, *The Code of the Drum*, *Eye on Ancient Egypt*, and *A Pirate Tale*.

Image credits

Cover Design: Nancy L. Roll, Michael A. Aspengren
Book Design: Nancy L. Roll, Deborah Lea Bell

Image Credits: ArtToday(some images copyright www.arttoday.com) pp. 5, 6, 7, 8, 9, 10, 12, 13, 14, 15, 16, 17, 18, 19, 20, 21, 22, 23, 24, 25, 26, 27, 28, 29, 30, 31, 32, 33, 34, 35, 36, 37, 38, 39, 40, 41, 42, 43, 45, 46, 47, 48, 49. 50; Corel pp. 3, 4, 11; NOAA p. 44; Northwind Picture Archives p. 22

Art Resource: Cover

© 2002 Perfection Learning®
First ebook edition 2012
www.perfectionlearning.com

6 7 8 9 PP 17 16 15 14

38568
PB ISBN: 978-0-7891-5621-1
RLB ISBN: 978-0-7569-0457-9
eISBN: 978-1-6138-4748-0

Printed in the United States of America

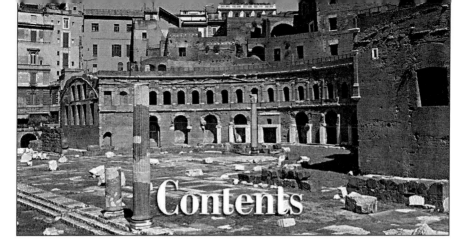

Contents

Introduction: Step into Ancient Rome 4

1. The Birth of a Great City............... 5

2. Growth, Power, and Prosperity 12

3. Everyday Life at a Glance............. 15

4. Growing Up Roman.................... 28

5. Roman Rituals 32

6. Blood Sports at the Colosseum 36

7. Natural Disaster Strikes Pompeii 39

8. Julius Caesar........................... 45

Conclusion: Back to the Future 50

Glossary.................................. 51

Index..................................... 56

Incubator Grant 16.01

Introduction

Step into Ancient Rome

Ancient Rome existed between 753 B.C. and 476 A.D. That was a long time ago! How do we know about ancient Rome?

Modern research tells us much about ancient times and people. **Artifacts** have been discovered. From them, we can learn a lot about how people lived.

Some information, such as exact locations and dates, is based on **educated guesses**. **Archaeologists** and other **scholars** make such guesses.

We know many things. However, we will never know every detail of ancient life. That's what makes what we *do* know so interesting. And that's what drives people to try to learn even more.

Keep that in mind as you step into ancient Rome.

Chapter 1

The Birth of a Great City

The Legend of Romulus and Remus

Many great civilizations have **legends** that explain how they came to be. These stories are passed from one generation to the next.

This one about Rome's creation has been told since the 4th century B.C. It has survived nearly 25 centuries!

The story of Rome's creation is a legend. People don't know for sure how Romulus came to be king. But it has long been accepted that he really was the first king of Rome.

The Creation of Rome

Brothers Romulus and Remus were twins. They had a human mother. Their father was Mars, the god of war.

King Amulius gave orders to kill the boys. He was afraid of them. You see, they were the rightful **heirs** *to his throne.*

Amulius would do anything to be king. Killing the princes was an easy choice for the cruel man.

The infants were placed in a basket. Then they were thrown into the Tiber River. Surely they would drown, starve, or freeze to death.

The king was happy. He gave the twins no more thought. The basket, however, would soon reach safety.

The river flooded. The basket floated to a shallow pool. It stuck in the roots of a fig tree on the riverbank.

A female wolf heard the babies crying. She followed the sounds to the boys.

She licked the mud off them. Then she stood guard until a shepherd came along.

The shepherd took the babies home. His wife was overjoyed. The couple raised the boys as their own.

The twins grew up in a happy, loving home. They became smart, strong, and brave men.

Eventually, Romulus and Remus left home. First, they killed Amulius. Then they decided to build a city. Where should it be? Along the Tiber, of course.

Romulus said, "I know the perfect place for our city. Let's build it on the spot where our basket washed up."

"That would be fine," said Remus. "Let's find the fig tree that saved us."

Romulus was sure that he had found the tree. It was on the Palatine Hill. Remus, however, was certain the tree was on the Aventine Hill.

They looked for signs to tell them where to build. Remus saw six vultures at Aventine. Romulus saw 12 vultures at Palatine. The brothers then knew that Palatine was the right place.

8

But the brothers had a terrible fight. Each wanted to be king.

Finally, the people chose Romulus. Remus was angry and hurt.

Romulus began building his city. The first stone was laid on a shepherds' holiday. It was April 21, 753 B.C.

Within weeks, a great wall circled the city. King Romulus was very proud. He ordered his subjects to use the city's gates whenever they came and went.

"No one shall jump over our walls," he said. "Not even our own people."

Remus was still upset at not being named king. He decided to annoy Romulus.

He jumped over the great wall. As he did, he cried, "It is so easy to jump over this wall! It will never protect the city!"

The Seven Kings of Rome

Seven kings ruled Rome between 753 B.C. and the founding of the Republic in 509 B.C.

- Romulus
  ruled 753–715 B.C.

- Numa Pompilius
  ruled 715–673 B.C.

- Tullus Hostilius
  ruled 673–641 B.C.

- Ancus Marcius
  ruled 641–616 B.C.

- Tarquinius Priscus
  ruled 616–579 B.C.

- Servius Tullius
  ruled 579–534 B.C.

- Tarquinius Superbus
  ruled 534–509 B.C.

Romulus was very angry. He chased after Remus with a pickax. He soon caught him. Blinded with rage, Romulus killed his own brother.

*King Romulus named his new city Rome. He named it after himself. His **reign** lasted nearly 40 years.*

Ruins of ancient Rome

Chapter

Growth, Power, and Prosperity

Roman villages first formed on the seven hills along the Tiber River. The Greeks lived nearby in southern Italy. The Etruscans lived to the north.

Kings ruled Rome for nearly two and a half centuries. This form of government is called a *monarchy*. The monarchy was overthrown in 509 B.C. A republican form of government replaced it.

Members of the **Senate** were the lawmakers. They elected two **consuls** to rule the **Republic**. Wealthy males were the only citizens allowed to vote.

The Romans wanted more territory. So they **conquered** their neighbors. They ruled the entire Italian **peninsula** by the middle of the 3rd century B.C.

Rome survived a century of brutal wars. Then it defeated Carthage in North Africa. This happened in 146 B.C. Carthage was a major overseas trading center.

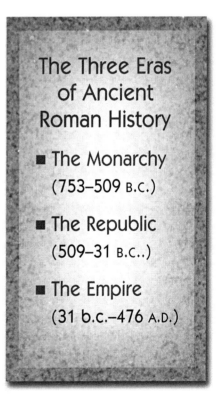

The Three Eras of Ancient Roman History

- The Monarchy (753–509 B.C.)

- The Republic (509–31 B.C..)

- The Empire (31 b.c.–476 A.D.)

Rome was now the most powerful city on the Mediterranean Sea. It was also among the richest.

Soon, a time of unrest became a civil war. People fought for control of the Republic. Julius Caesar emerged as ruler in 45 B.C.

After Caesar's death, his nephew, Octavian, took over. He was the first Roman emperor. Octavian was later called Augustus.

Julius Caesar

The Roman army continued seizing land around the Mediterranean. Eventually, the Roman **Empire** reached far north to Britain.

Rome was not built in a day.

Have you ever heard that saying? People usually say that when they have a big job to do.

The great city of Rome took shape over many centuries. It took patience, hard work, and **sacrifice**.

The saying helps people remember that their own tasks will take time.

Chapter

Everyday Life at a Glance

Baths

Public baths were popular Roman gathering places. Men went to the baths often. They went to meet friends, play games, and get clean. They usually went after working.

Some towns had separate women's baths. In other towns, women went to the men's baths in the morning.

The Roman "bath" was quite different from a modern bath. Nobody used soap. People spread olive oil on their skin. Then they relaxed in a steamy room. The process opened the **pores**. Afterward, the people plunged into a cold pool to close their pores.

Slaves tended the fires outside the bathhouses. They kept the fires burning all day. The heat traveled under the floors and through the walls.

Clothing

Roman men wore gowns, or *togas*. They were usually white. The emperor's, however, was purple. Gray or black togas were worn during times of **mourning**.

A toga was a 7-foot by 18-foot rectangular cloth draped about the body. It was difficult to keep togas in place. Slaves were often seen helping their owners adjust their togas.

Very few women wore togas. Some did, but it was frowned upon.

Women were more likely to wear gowns and cloaks. These were made of wool or linen. Wealthy women wore Indian cotton and Chinese silk.

Both men and women wore sandals. And everyone wore wooden clogs in the baths. Otherwise, their feet would burn on the hot floors!

Catacomb

Death and Burial

Ancient Romans honored their dead.
Sometimes, they burned, or *cremated*, bodies.
Then they kept the ashes on display in **urns**.

Other Romans buried the dead in marble
coffins. For a while, these were placed outside
the city walls. The coffins lined the roads
leading up to the city. Later, the Romans
created underground *catacombs*, or tunnels.
The coffins were then kept there.

The Forum

Nearly every Roman city was built around a forum. The forum housed the main marketplace. It was usually an open square surrounded by columns or pillars.

Buildings outside the forum often included

- government buildings
- public baths
- shops
- temples
- theaters

"There's nowhere a man can get any peace in Rome. Shouting schoolmasters wake you up at dawn. At night, it's the bakers. And all day long, it's the coppersmiths with their hammers."
—1st-century poet Martial

In the interest of health, **aqueducts** and sewers were built. They were added throughout the Empire. The aqueducts brought fresh water in. The sewers carried the old, or used, water out.

In the 1st century A.D., water flowed into Rome through nine hillside aqueducts. The system carried 222 million gallons of water every day!

Health and Medicine

Ancient Romans had short lives. Most people didn't live past the age of 50.

The practice of medicine was still new. People did not understand how disease spread. Doctors relied upon trial and error to help patients.

Only a few Romans could afford a doctor's help. The visits cost too much.

Homes

Most Romans lived in apartment houses. Some houses had shops on the ground floor. An expensive penthouse apartment might be at the top. Smaller apartments would fill in the rest of the building.

Not many apartments had bathrooms or kitchens. People carried in water from public fountains. And they ate mostly cold food or bought hot meals in shops.

Apartment houses were cheaply built. And they were likely to fall down. They frequently burned down too.

The wealthy lived in large, beautiful, solid houses. Outside was a large garden. There was a courtyard too. Inside were **mosaic** floors and colorfully painted walls.

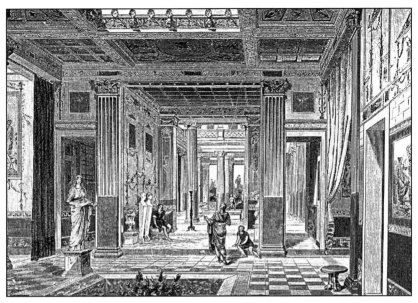
Atrium

The space inside the front door was the *atrium*. An opening in the ceiling let in sunlight and rain. The rainwater fell into a pool built in the floor.

Other rooms included

- bedrooms
- bathroom
- entertaining room
- library
- **shrine**
- storeroom

The Romans protected their homes with locks and keys. Most kept their money in strongboxes. Furniture was scarce in large houses as well as in small apartments.

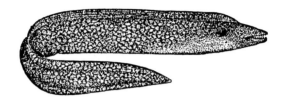

A Sampling
of Popular Food Items

- fish
- porridge
- olives
- cake
- sausage
- pigeon
- deer
- eel
- peacock
- ostrich
- oysters
- larks' tongues

- bread
- fresh fruit
- partridge
- hare
- donkey
- pig
- chicken
- wine
- dates
- eggs
- dove
- mice cooked in honey

Music

Romans loved music. It played an important part in religion, the theater, and the home. The many instruments played included

- cymbals

- double pipes

- flute

- panpipe

- spiral horn

- tuba—this looked nothing like a modern tuba

- water organ

Writing

Very few ancient Roman texts exist today. We know, however, that Romans spread vast amounts of information across their empire. They wrote on scrolls, buildings, sculptures, monuments, and coins.

Books and legal contracts were written with pen and ink on **parchment** or **papyrus**.

For simple notes, Romans scratched writing onto beeswax tablets with a sharpened stick. This writing tool was called a *stylus*. People could then "erase" their writing with the blunt end of the stick.

They Didn't Even Have Spray Paint . . .

Would you believe that **graffiti** was common in ancient Rome? Most buildings and walls, including homes, were covered with painted or scratched-on messages. Today, graffiti is considered an act of **vandalism**.

Example of Roman Graffiti

Auge is in love with Arabienus

Everyday People

What jobs did people have in ancient Rome? If you lived then, you might meet these people on the street. Do you see any that you would be surprised to meet today?

acrobat	**gladiator**	ruler
actor	goldsmith	senator
banker	juggler	slave
barber	lawyer	**snake charmer**
builder	**mariner**	soldier
butcher	**midwife**	**spinner**
camel farmer	**mime**	street singer
candle maker	peacock farmer	surgeon
cobbler	perfumer	tax collector
dentist	potter	teacher
fishmonger	poultry picker	writer
fortune-teller	priestess	

Chapter 4

Growing Up Roman

Children in Rome did many of the same things kids do today. They went to school. They made up games. They played with dolls, marbles, and toy chariots. They sang and danced. They thought about what they'd do when they grew up.

There is one big difference, though. Roman children often struck out on their own very early. They did not get to stay "kids" for very long. Some started working as early as age eight. Others were married by age 12!

What about school? Education was thought of as a **privilege**. It was far more likely for a child to *not* go to school.

Children from wealthy families often had their own teachers. These teachers might be educated slaves or **freedmen**. Parents expected the teachers to take over a child's education when the child turned three or four years old.

Some children were sent to school outside the home. They usually started at age seven. All of the kids learned from the same teacher in the same class setting. The school day began at dawn and ended at noon.

You might find a teacher, or *magister*, holding class outside, just off the busy street. He would set up his classroom under a shop's awning.

Students sat at desks on stools facing the teacher's chair. The only subjects covered were reading, writing, and arithmetic. Necessary classroom supplies included

- **abacuses**
- blackboard
- washbasin

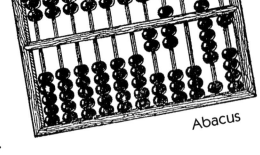
Abacus

Every eighth day was a school holiday. Students had no school for five days after every full moon.

Roman girls attended school from ages 7 to 13. Then they studied household functions. Their mothers trained them for marriage.

Boys attended school from ages 7 to 15. The lucky ones continued their studies in government or law. Others went straight to work and started families of their own.

In ancient Rome, children could become legally engaged at age 7. Girls could marry at 12. And boys could marry at 14. Parents often arranged their children's marriages.

5

Roman Rituals

Religious rituals were important to early Romans. Each household contained a shrine. It was called a *lararium*. Families worshiped at the shrine every day.

Daily ceremonies honored gods and spirits. Family members who had died were also remembered.

Often, someone poured wine, milk, or oil over a fire on the altar.

Jupiter

The Roman gods Jupiter, Juno, Minerva, and Mars were Rome's protectors. Families held special services to keep the gods happy.

Romans had adopted the Greek gods as their own. They gave them different names, though. For example, the Greek god Eros is the Roman god Cupid.

Roman Gods

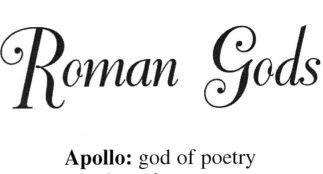

Apollo: god of poetry and music

Ceres: goddess of the earth

Cupid: god of love

Diana: goddess of the hunt

Faunus: god of fields and shepherds

Flora: goddess of flowers

Juno: queen of the gods

Jupiter: king of the gods

Luna: goddess of the moon

Mars: god of war

Mercury: messenger of the gods

34

and Goddesses

Minerva: goddess of wisdom

Mors: god of death

Neptune: god of the oceans

Pluto: god of the underworld

Proserpina: goddess of the underworld

Psyche: goddess of the soul

Somnus: god of sleep

Venus: goddess of love and beauty

Vesta: goddess of the hearth

Victoria: goddess of victory

Vulcan: god of fire

Minerva

Pluto

Chapter 6

Blood Sports
at the Colosseum

Rome's Colosseum is considered an engineering masterpiece. The emperor Titus built it in 80 A.D.

It was built so the people of Rome could watch popular "games." In these games, gladiators fought to the death.

The arena was huge. It held 50,000 people. They could come in through 80 entrances. A sand floor soaked up fighters' blood.

In the early days, the Colosseum could be filled with water. Emperors hosted "sea battles." Gladiators fought one another in boats.

Many people turned their slaves into gladiators. Some gladiators even attended special training schools.

Sometimes, gladiators fought in circuses. Instead of fighting other men, they fought— and brutally killed—animals. Romans loved these blood sports.

Some gladiators became rich and famous. They had many fans.

Another common Colosseum "show" was the killing of a criminal. A criminal would be tied up in the middle of the arena floor. Then a bull or a  bear would be released. People cheered to see the criminal gored or mauled to death.

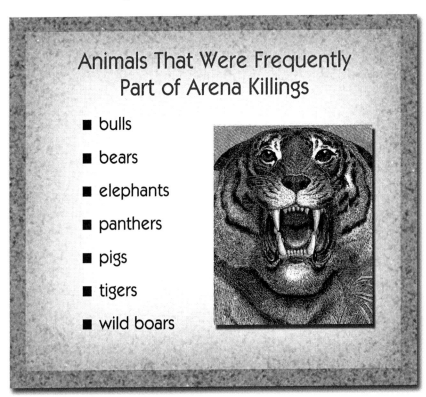

Animals That Were Frequently Part of Arena Killings

- bulls
- bears
- elephants
- panthers
- pigs
- tigers
- wild boars

Chapter

Natural Disaster Strikes Pompeii

Remains of the ancient Roman city of Pompeii tell us a lot about life back then. The "lost" city was discovered in the 18th century. It was dug up in the 19th century.

In 79 A.D., Pompeii was a busy town. It was on the Bay of Naples, south of Rome. Olive oil, wine, fish sauce, and perfume were produced there.

What happened to Pompeii? What was that last day like?

Pompeii market

The Beginning of the End

The morning air was brisk. The sky was bright and clear. People bustled about the city as usual. They had no way of knowing what the day would bring.

Farmers worked their fields. Shop owners went about their business. Lawmakers discussed important local issues.

Servants cleaned houses. Cooks prepared meals.

Children laughed and played outside. Some people made plans for the future. Others simply went about enjoying the day.

At noon, citizens gasped. They heard a sharp, violent thunderclap. Many thought an earthquake would follow.

Those who looked toward Mt. Vesuvius knew that something else was happening. A giant cloud burst into the air. Fire lit up the sky. The volcano had **erupted**!

Mt. Vesuvius

False Night

Ashes fell from the cloud. Suddenly, a false night settled over the city. It was the middle of the day. But the sky was as black as coal.

Fear set in. People panicked. Many tried to run away. They didn't have enough time. Most people decided to seek shelter.

Soon the city was pelted with burning lava and rock. A seemingly endless storm dumped 13 feet of ash on the ground.

People were struck down in the streets. Horses caught on fire. Buildings collapsed.

Those who had reached shelter listened to the horrifying sounds of death and destruction. They clung to one another. They prayed for a miracle. Some even prayed for death. They wished for anything to stop the nightmare.

Pliny the Younger wrote about the tragic end to Pompeii around 97–109 A.D. He saw the eruption—but from a distance. Here's what he wrote.

"You could hear the shrieks of women, the wailing of infants, and the shouting of men. Some were calling their parents, others their children or their wives . . . Many asked the help of the gods. But still more imagined there were no gods left, and that the universe was plunged into eternal darkness forever."

Calm Is Restored

The eruption went on for 19 terrible hours.

At 7 A.M. the next day, strong winds blew through the streets of Pompeii. The gusts dropped a final layer of volcanic ash on the city. Everything—people, animals, houses, shops, the forum—was completely buried.

Toxic gases settled over the ash. They seeped into open airways. The scorching heat was awful.

When it all ended, Pompeii was finally at peace.

Almost half of the city of Pompeii remains buried today.

About 2,000 people died in the eruption of Mt. Vesuvius.

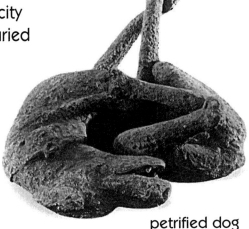

petrified dog

Julius Caesar

Can you name one important person from ancient Roman history? If you can, it's likely to be Julius Caesar. He is one of the most well-known historical figures. People have studied and written about him for centuries.

Julius Caesar was born on July 12, 100 B.C., in Rome. His mother was Aurelia. She was a guiding force in Caesar's life. His father was Gaius. He died when Caesar was 16.

Caesar became a great Roman general. He fought in civil wars and was known as a great warrior.

He sought election to public office at an early age. He won a small post in 86 B.C. He was just 14 years old!

Caesar was brave and very tough. Pirates captured him in the winter of 75–74 B.C. They demanded ransom money. As they waited for it, Caesar threatened to **crucify** them. And he did just that as soon as he was released.

After the ordeal, he returned to Rome. He wanted to pursue a career in politics.

Over the years, Caesar held many offices. He was an important political figure. He became Rome's ruler in 48 B.C. His title was **dictator**. He created a strong and powerful land.

Caesar had many enemies in the Senate. They feared that he would become king. So they decided to stop him.

On March 15, 44 B.C., Caesar entered the Senate. He was attacked and stabbed 23 times. A group of 60 senators had plotted his death.

After Caesar's death, civil war raged in Rome for 13 years.

March 15 was known as the Ides of March.

Fast Facts About Julius Caesar

- His **motto** was *"Veni, vidi, vici."* In English, that means "I came, I saw, I conquered."

- The month of July is named after him.

- He introduced the leap year.

- During his reign, he supplied 150,000 poor families with free corn.

- He married three times.

- He had one child—a daughter named Julia.

- He wrote more than a dozen books. His writings included **memoirs**, histories, joke collections, poetry, and grammar studies.

- His death was the subject of a 1589 play by William Shakespeare.

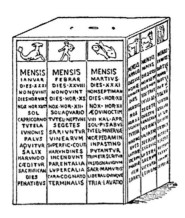

Caesar and Our Calendar

The Roman calendar originated in Egypt. In 45 B.C. Caesar changed the calendar year from 355 days to 365 days. That's how long it takes the earth to revolve around the sun.

The system became known as the Julian calendar. We use the same calendar today.

The Romans used these names for the 12 months.

Ianuarius	Quintilis (later changed to Iulius)
Februarius	Sextilis (later changed to Augustus)
Martius	September
Aprilis	October
Maius	November
Iunius	December

Conclusion

Back to the Future

The events in this book took place as long as 2,700 years ago. Think for a moment what life will be like 2,700 years from today. What do you think kids in the 56th century A.D. will learn about you?

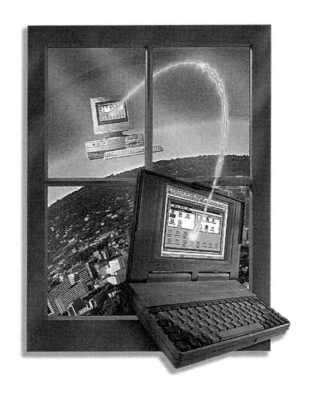

Glossary

abacus
ancient calculator that uses stones to count

aqueduct
structure built to carry water

archaeologist
one who studies past civilizations

artifact
something made by humans in an earlier time period

cobbler
maker of shoes and other leather goods

conquer
to overcome with force

consul
leader who sees laws are obeyed and justice is served

crucify
to put someone to death by nailing him or her to a large wooden cross

dictator	person granted total power
educated guess	guess based on knowledge about a topic
empire	group of countries ruled by one nation
erupt	to force out or release suddenly
fishmonger	merchant who sells fish
freedman	former slave who either bought his freedom or was set free
gladiator	one who fights to the death for public entertainment
graffiti	writing on a public surface
heir	one who receives money, property, or a title when a relative dies

legend	story that's passed down over many years
mariner	sailor
memoir	writings about personal experience
midwife	one who helps women with childbirth
mime	entertainer who acts out scenes from life without talking
mosaic	having small tiles laid in patterns
motto	sentence or phrase expressing a thought to live by
mourning	period of time in which respect is shown to someone who has died

papyrus	plant materials used to write on
parchment	dried skin of a sheep or a goat used to write on
peninsula	land surrounded by water on three sides
pore	tiny opening in the skin
privilege	honor or right for only a chosen few
reign	length of time a king or queen rules
republic	state in which power is held by the people instead of by one person only
sacrifice	loss; act of giving up something to gain something else

scholar	one who has knowledge
Senate	the group of people who governed Rome
shrine	special place set aside for worship
slave	someone owned by and forced to work for another person
snake charmer	entertainer who works with snakes
spinner	one who joins fibers into thread for sewing
toxic	poisonous
urn	vaselike jar
vandalism	senseless destruction of public or private property

Index

Aventine Hill, 8

Caesar, Julius, 14, 45–49

Colosseum, 36–38

gladiators, 27, 36–37

King Amulius, 6–8

Mt. Vesuvius, 41–44

Octavian (Augustus), 14

Palatine Hill, 8

Pompeii, 39–44

Remus, 6–10

Roman life

    baths, 15–16, 17

    calendar, 49

    clothing, 17

    death and burial, 18, 32

education, 28–31

food, 23

forum, 19

gods, 6, 32, 33–35

health and medicine, 20

homes, 21–22

music, 24

occupations, 27

rituals, 32–33

sports, 36–38

writing, 25–26

Romulus, 5, 6–10, 11

Senate, 12-13, 47

seven kings, 10